DISCARDED

A
Singing
Wind

A Singing Wind

Selected Poems by
JAMES STEPHENS

Edited by
QUAIL HAWKINS

Drawings by
HAROLD GOODWIN

THE MACMILLAN COMPANY, NEW YORK

INTRODUCTION

"Great men do go out of date pretty fast. Young people tend to imagine that everybody over forty-five years of age died a couple of years before Columbus discovered America," said James Stephens in one of his broadcasts over the BBC in 1944. He would probably not be surprised to know that young people of today don't trust anybody over thirty. But the good poetry written by poets of the past who created it before they were thirty still speaks across the years to the young of today.

Most of these poems were written by James Stephens while he was a young man. He speaks to the young in heart who are concerned with love, loneliness, life and death, beauty and ugliness, and the whole natural world around us.

Stephens was an Irishman whose birth date is a subject of some mystery. It is generally given as February 9, 1880, but James Joyce, Stephens' very good friend, always insisted they were both born in Dublin on February 2, 1882. (For this reason as well as his faith in Stephens' ability, Joyce considered having Stephens finish *Finnegans Wake* if he, Joyce, were physically unable to do so.)

Although a great man, Stephens was not a big man. He was about four feet ten inches tall, with a large head, and a shock of black hair that gave him the look of a frightened leprechaun. He says this about himself in *James, Seumas and Jacques:* "Before I turned over a new leaf and became a poet . . . I was a gymnast. I was short and light and strong and seventeen years of age, and there's nothing better than that except to be tall and heavy and stronger and twenty years of age. . . . I wasn't bad at the game and in my second year our team won the championship of Ireland, and I was on it."

Stephens claimed that his size was the reason he became a writer. He said his first job was driving a horse and cart around Dublin, and he couldn't stand the contempt of the horses for one who had to stand on a box to harness them. Writing was the only work he thought he could do in which his height was of no importance.

His early life must have been unpleasant in many ways, but for one born in poverty he was lucky, for at six years of age he was committed, for begging, to the Meath Protestant Industrial School for Boys. Quite possibly at this time he lost track of his family. The education given him in the school was excellent, and in addition he became an omnivorous reader. He says, "I loved reading, and I loved eating, and to do these two things at the same time seemed to me to be the height of bliss. I loved reading so much that when I couldn't get a real book to read I would even read poetry. That happened to me one time. I had nothing to read, so I was reading the *Songs of Innocence* of William Blake, when, quite suddenly quite out of the blue, my mind whispered to me, 'I can do that.'

"I was delighted, as I always was when my mind condescended to notice that I was present. So I went to bed with a note-book and a pencil, and during that night of the nights I wrote twenty-five poems, and I could have written fifty but that morning had come, and I had to get up and go to work." It did not all come as easily, however. He said in another broadcast, "I once had to wait three years . . . to get the last line of another poem of four verses."

He supported himself as a clerk in a solicitor's office but he was not interested in the law. He was already writing and appeared for the first time in the *United Irishman* in 1905. He was soon involved in the Irish Revival, which sought to express Irish independence from England in literature as well as politics, and his poetry was regularly published in *Sinn Fein*.

In 1908 he was discovered by the Irish poet George Russell (known as Æ) and was gradually drawn into the famous Dublin literary group that included Yeats, Maud Gonne, Arthur Griffith, Padraic Colum, and Stephen MacKenna. In 1909 his book of poems,

Insurrections, was published. His *Hill of Vision*, poetry, as well as his prose works, *The Charwoman's Daughter* and his most famous book *The Crock of Gold*, were all published in 1912. By this time he was internationally famous.

Stephens left Ireland about 1925, first to live in France and later in England. When he left Dublin his source of inspiration seemed to dry up and his creative work largely ceased. He was greatly interested in theosophy and much of his poetry was influenced by this. He was also a famous conversationalist and for many years made broadcasts for the BBC as well as giving many lectures and poetry recitals, several times in the United States. He died in 1950.

This selection was made from Stephens' *Collected Poems*, Second Edition, With Added Material, published in 1957. The arrangement of the poems generally follows that of *Collected Poems*, including headings, with the exception of inclusions too few to be grouped under the original headings. These poems are listed under "Miscellany." I have tried to make a balanced choice to show how an Irish poet looked at life and death in the early twentieth century.

My thanks go to all the people who have encouraged and helped me in this project, especially Florence O. Jensen and her English classes at Alameda (California) High School, who commented on the poems; Sally Roberts Hawkins; Harvey Fergusson; and Shirley Dolgoff, my editor at Macmillan. Without their help I should have had a difficult rather than a joyous task in making this selection of poems.

Quail Hawkins

Berkeley, California
1968

CONTENTS

IN GREEN WAYS

A HONEYCOMB

IN THE TWO LIGHTS

HEELS AND HEAD

LESS THAN DAINTILY

THE GOLDEN BIRD

MISCELLANY

IN GREEN WAYS

THE GOAT PATHS

I

The crooked paths
Go every way
Upon the hill
—They wind about
Through the heather,
In and out
Of a quiet
Sunniness.

And the goats,
Day after day,
Stray
In sunny
Quietness;
Cropping here,
And cropping there
—As they pause,
And turn,
And pass—
Now a bit
Of heather spray,
Now a mouthful
Of the grass.

In the deeper
Sunniness;
In the place
Where nothing stirs;
Quietly
In quietness;
In the quiet
Of the furze
They stand a while;
They dream;
They lie;
They stare
Upon the roving sky.

If you approach
They run away!
They will stare,
And stamp,
And bound,
With a sudden angry sound,
To the sunny
Quietude;
To crouch again,
Where nothing stirs,
In the quiet
Of the furze:
To crouch them down again,
And brood,
In the sunny
Solitude.

3

Were I but
As free
As they,

I would stray
Away
And brood;
I would beat
A hidden way,
Through the quiet
Heather spray,
To a sunny
Solitude.

And should you come
I'd run away!
I would make an angry sound,
I would stare,
And stamp,
And bound
To the deeper
Quietude;
To the place
Where nothing stirs
In the quiet
Of the furze.

4

In that airy
Quietness
I would dream
As long as they:
Through the quiet
Sunniness
I would stray
Away
And brood,
All among
The heather spray,
In a sunny
Solitude.

—I would think
Until I found
Something
I can never find;
—Something
Lying
On the ground,
In the bottom
Of my mind.

FOLLOW, FOLLOW, FOLLOW

Follow! Follow! Follow!
Blackbird, thrush and swallow!
The air is soft, the sun is dancing through
The dancing boughs;
A little while me company along
And I will go with you.
Arouse! Arouse!
Among the leaves I sing my pleasant song.

Sky! Sky! On high! O gentle majesty!
Come all ye happy birds and follow, follow!
Under the slender interlacing boughs,
Blackbird, thrush and swallow!
No longer in the sunlight sit and drowse
But me accompany along;
No longer be ye mute!
Arouse! Arouse!
Among the leaves I sing my pleasant song.

Lift, lift, ye happy birds! Lift song and wing;
And sing and fly; and fly again, and sing
Up to the very blueness of the sky
Your happy words!
O Follow! Follow! Follow!

Where we go racing through the shady ways,
Blackbird, thrush and swallow,
Shouting aloud our ecstasy of praise!
Under the slender interlacing boughs
Me company along;
The sun is coming with us!
Rouse! O rouse!
Among the leaves I sing my pleasant song.

MINUETTE

I

The moon shines,
And the wind blows,
And the heart knows,

Carelessly, and carelessly!
That to them each thing inclines,
And that everything is free!

All that is, is given to thee!
Take the love, that comes and goes!
Uncomplaining, thankless, be,

As the moon, the bird, the rose,
Thankless, uncomplaining, are
Beauty, Music, and a Star!

II

Call, and come, and come, and call!
Nothing is denied the gay!
All to each, and each to all.

Fall, and flow, and go away;
As the moon shines, and the heart knows;
Carelessly, as the wind blows!

Not for duty we fulfil
Lovely motions—'tis for naught!
All the will of good and ill,

All of ignorance, and thought,
All are harmless, if we are
Free as Wind, and Rose, and Star.

III

Taking all of cherishing
That befall, or may not fall,
As a happy, chancing, thing,

Some for each, and all for all;
Taking all the haps that be,
Carelessly, and carelessly!

Life comes on, with not a word;
Love is love, on no demand;
Death, unasked, hath him bestirred,

Lifting all up by the hand:
All that fall he stoops above
Lovingly, for he is Love!

IV

Love is round, and round, and round!
Everywhere, in every spot,
It is lost, and it is found,

Here it is—and here is not!
Man, and beast, and bird, and snake,
Take, and take, and take, and take,

As the Moon takes up the sight!
As the Rose takes up the shower!
As the Heart takes all Delight,

Might and Beauty for its dower!
All that is—for all is free—
Take carelessly, and carelessly!

THE RIVALS

I heard a bird at dawn
Singing sweetly on a tree,
That the dew was on the lawn,
And the wind was on the lea;
But I didn't listen to him,
For he didn't sing to me!

I didn't listen to him,
For he didn't sing to me
That the dew was on the lawn,
And the wind was on the lea!
I was singing at the time,
Just as prettily as he!

I was singing all the time,
Just as prettily as he,
About the dew upon the lawn,
And the wind upon the lea!
So I didn't listen to him,
As he sang upon a tree!

AND IT WAS
WINDY WEATHER

Now the winds are riding by;
Clouds are galloping the sky;

Bush and tree are lashing bare,
Savage, boughs on savage air;

Crying, as they lash and sway,
—Pull the roots out of the clay!

Lift away: away:
Away!

Leave security, and speed
From the root, the mud, the mead!

Into sea and air, we go!
To chase the gull, the moon!—and know

—Flying high!
Flying high!—

All the freedom of the sky!
All the freedom of the sky!

DANCE

1

Left and right and swing around!
Soar and dip and fall for glee!
Happy sky, and bird, and ground!
Happy wind, and happy tree!

Happy minions, dancing mad!
Joy is guide enough for you;
Cure the world of good and bad;
And teach us innocence anew!

Good and bad and right and wrong!
Wave the silly words away!
This is wisdom—to be strong!
This is virtue—to be gay!

Let us sing and dance, until
We shall know the final art;
How to banish good and ill
With the laughter of the heart!

THE CENTAURS

Playing upon the hill three centaurs were!
They lifted each a hoof! They stared at me!
And stamped the dust!

They stamped the dust! They snuffed upon the air!
And all their movements had the fierce glee
Of power, and pride, and lust!

Of power and pride and lust! Then, with a shout,
They tossed their heads, and wheeled, and galloped round,
In furious brotherhood!

In furious brotherhood! Around, about,
They charged, they swerved, they leaped! Then, bound on bound,
They raced into the wood!

THE CRACKLING TWIG

There came a satyr creeping through the wood,
His hair fell on his breast, his legs were slim:
His eyes were dancing wickedly, he stood,
He peeped about on every side of him.

He danced! He peeped! But, at a sound I made,
A crackling twig, he turned; and, suddenly,
In three great jumps, he bounded to the shade,
And disappeared among the greenery!

IN THE NIGHT

There always is a noise when it is dark!
It is the noise of silence, and the noise
Of blindness!

The noise of silence, and the noise of blindness
Do frighten me!
They hold me stark and rigid as a tree!

These frighten me!
These hold me stark and rigid as a tree!
Because at last their tumult is more loud
Than thunder!

Because at last
Their tumult is more loud than thunder,
They terrify my soul! They tear
My heart asunder!

THE SNARE

I hear a sudden cry of pain!
There is a rabbit in a snare:
Now I hear the cry again,
But I cannot tell from where.

But I cannot tell from where
He is calling out for aid!
Crying on the frightened air,
Making everything afraid!

Making everything afraid!
Wrinkling up his little face!
As he cries again for aid;
—And I cannot find the place!

And I cannot find the place
Where his paw is in the snare!
Little One! Oh, Little One!
I am searching everywhere!

LITTLE THINGS

Little things, that run, and quail,
And die, in silence and despair!

Little things, that fight, and fail,
And fall, on sea, and earth, and air!

All trapped and frightened little things,
The mouse, the coney, hear our prayer!

As we forgive those done to us,
—The lamb, the linnet, and the hare—

Forgive us all our trespasses,
Little creatures, everywhere!

CHILL OF THE EVE

A long green swell
Slopes soft to the sea;
And a far-off bell
Swings sweet to me;
As the grey
Chill day
Slips away
From the lea.

Spread cold and far,
Without one glow
From a mild pale star,
Is the sky's steel bow;
And the grey
Chill day
Slips away
Below.

Yon green tree grieves
To the air around;
And the whispering leaves
Have a lonely sound;
As the grey
Chill day

Slips away
From the ground.

And dark, more dark,
The shades settle down;
Far off is a spark
From the lamp-lit town;
And the grey
Chill day
Slips away
With a frown.

THE SHELL

I

And then I pressed the shell
Close to my ear,
And listened well.

And straightway, like a bell,
Came low and clear
The slow, sad, murmur of far distant seas

Whipped by an icy breeze
Upon a shore
Wind-swept and desolate.

It was a sunless strand that never bore
The footprint of a man.
Nor felt the weight

Since time began
Of any human quality or stir,
Save what the dreary winds and wave incur.

And in the hush of waters was the sound
Of pebbles, rolling round;
For ever rolling, with a hollow sound:

And bubbling sea-weeds, as the waters go,
Swish to and fro
Their long cold tentacles of slimy grey:

There was no day;
Nor ever came a night
Setting the stars alight

To wonder at the moon:
Was twilight only, and the frightened croon,
Smitten to whimpers, of the dreary wind

And waves that journeyed blind . . .
And then I loosed my ear—Oh, it was sweet
To hear a cart go jolting down the street.

THE MAIN-DEEP

The long-rólling,
Steady-póuring,
Deep-trenchéd
Green billów:

The wide-topped,
Unbróken,
Green-glacid,
Slow-sliding,

Cold-flushing,
—On—on—on—
Chill-rushing,
Hush—hushing,

. . . Hush—hushing . . .

A HONEYCOMB

MARY HYNES

1

She is the sky
Of the sun!
She is the dart
Of love!

She is the love
Of my heart!
She is a rune!
She is above

The women
Of the race of Eve
As the sun
Is above the moon!

2

Lovely and airy
The view from the hill
That looks down
Ballylea!

But no good sight
Is good, until
By great good luck
You see

The Blossom
Of the Branches,
Walking towards you,
Airily!

THE WOOD OF FLOWERS

I went to the Wood of Flowers,
No one went with me;
I was there alone for hours;
I was happy as could be,
In the Wood of Flowers!

There was grass
On the ground;
There were leaves
On the tree;

And the wind
Had a sound
Of such sheer
Gaiety,

That I
Was as happy
As happy could be,
In the Wood of Flowers!

PEGGY MITCHELL

As lily grows up easily,
In modest, gentle dignity,
To sweet perfection,
—So grew she,
As easily!

Or as the rose,
That takes no care,
Will open out, on sunny air,
Bloom after bloom,
Fair after fair;
Just so did she
—As carelessly!

She is our torment without end!
She is our enemy, our friend!
Our joy, our woe!
And she will send
Madness, or glee,
To you, or me,
—And endlessly!

SWEET APPLE

At the end of the bough!
At the top of the tree!
—As fragrant, as high,
And as lovely, as thou—
One sweet apple reddens,
Which all men may see,
—At the end of the bough!

Swinging full to the view!
Though the harvesters now
Overlook it, repass it,
And pass busily:
Overlook it!
Nay, pluck it!
They do not know how!

For it swings out of reach
Like a cloud! And as free
As a star; or thy beauty,
That seems too, I vow,
Remote as the sweet apple, swinging
—Ah me!
At the end of the bough!

THE CANAL BANK

I know a girl,
And a girl knows me,
And the owl says, what!
And the owl says, who?

But what we know
We both agree
That nobody else
Shall hear or see;

It's all between herself and me:
To wit? said the owl,
To woo! said I,
To-what! To-wit! To-woo!

THE COOLIN

Come with me, under my coat,
And we will drink our fill
Of the milk of the white goat,
Or wine if it be thy will.

And we will talk, until
Talk is a trouble, too,
Out on the side of the hill;
And nothing is left to do,

But an eye to look into an eye;
And a hand in a hand to slip;
And a sigh to answer a sigh;
And a lip to find out a lip!

What if the night be black!
Or the air on the mountain chill!
Where the goat lies down in her track,
And all but the fern is still!

Stay with me, under my coat!
And we will drink our fill
Of the milk of the white goat,
Out on the side of the hill!

THE DAISIES

In the scented bud of the morning-O,
When the windy grass went rippling far!
I saw my dear one walking slow
In the field where the daisies are.

We did not laugh, and we did not speak,
As we wandered happily, to and fro;
I kissed my dear on either cheek,
In the bud of the morning-O!

A lark sang up, from the breezy land;
A lark sang down, from a cloud afar;
As she and I went, hand in hand,
In the field where the daisies are.

THE BUDS

Now I can see
The buds are green again
On every tree.

Through the dear intercourse of sun and dew,
Of thrilling root, and folding earth, anew
They come, in beauty.

They up to the sun,
As on a breast, are lifting every one
Green leaves.

Under the eaves
The sparrows and the swallows
Are in love.

There is a chatter in the woods above,
Where the grim crow
Is telling what his sweetheart wants to know.

For the sun
Is shining fair,
And the green
Is on the tree;

And the wind
Is everywhere
Whispering
So urgently!

You will die
Unless you do
Find a mate
To whisper to.

GREEN WEEDS

To be not jealous, give not love!
Rate not thy fair all fair above,
Or thou'lt be decked in green, the hue
That jealousy is bounden to.

That lily hand! Those lips of fire!
Those dewy eyes that spill desire!
Those mounds of lambent snow, may be
Found anywhere it pleaseth thee

To turn! Then turn, and be not mad
Though all of loveliness she had:
—She hath not *all* of loveliness!
A store remains, wherewith to bless

The bee, the bird, the butterfly,
And thou! Go, search with those that fly
For that, which thou shalt easy find
On every path, and any wind!

Nor dream that she be Seal and Star
Who is but as her sisters are!
And whose reply is, Yes and No,
To all that come, and all that go.

—I love!—Then love again, my friend;
Enjoy thy love, without an end!—
—I love . . . Ah, cease! Know what is what,
Thou dost not love, if she love not!

For if thou truly lovéd her
From thee away she could not stir!
But ever at thy side, would be
Thy self, and thy felicity!

Go! Drape thee in the greeny hue!
Thou art not Love! She is not True!
And, no more need be said—Adieu!

DEIRDRE

Do not let any woman read this verse!
It is for men, and after them their sons,
And their sons' sons!

The time comes when our hearts sink utterly;
When we remember Deirdre, and her tale,
And that her lips are dust.

Once she did tread the earth: men took her hand;
They looked into her eyes and said their say,
And she replied to them.

More than two thousand years it is since she
Was beautiful: she trod the waving grass;
She saw the clouds.

Two thousand years! The grass is still the same;
The clouds as lovely as they were that time
When Deirdre was alive.

But there has been again no woman born
Who was so beautiful; not one so beautiful
Of all the women born.

Let all men go apart and mourn together!
No man can ever love her! Not a man
Can dream to be her lover!

No man can bend before her! No man say—
What could one say to her? There are no words
That one could say to her!

Now she is but a story that is told
Beside the fire! No man can ever be
The friend of that poor queen!

FOSSILS

And then she saw me creeping!
Saw and stood
Transfixed upon the fringes of the wood,
And straight went, leaping!

Headlong, down the pitch
Of the curved hill!
Over the ditch,
And through the skirt of bushes by the rill
She pelted screaming!

Swerved from the water, sideways, with a twist,
Just as I clutched,
And missed!

Flashed white beneath my hand, and doubled back,
Swift as a twisting hare upon the track,
Hot for the hill again!
But all in vain!

Her hair swung far behind!
Straight as a stream balanced upon the wind!
Oh, it was black! Dipped
In the dregs of midnight, with a spark
Caught from a star that smouldered in the dark!

It I gripped!
Drew for a moment tight!
Jerked, with a victor's cry,
Down in the grasses high
Her to the hot brown earth and threatened—daft—

And then!
. . . She laughed!

THE RED-HAIRED MAN'S WIFE

I have taken that vow!
And you were my friend
But yesterday—Now
All that's at an end;
And you are my husband, and claim me, and I must depend!

Yesterday I was free!
Now you, as I stand,
Walk over to me
And take hold of my hand;
You look at my lips! Your eyes are too bold, your smile is too bland!

My old name is lost;
My distinction of race!
Now, the line has been crossed,
Must I step to your pace?
Must I walk as you list, and obey, and smile up in your face?

All the white and the red
Of my cheeks you have won!
All the hair of my head!
And my feet, tho' they run,
Are yours, and you own me and end me, just as I begun!

Must I bow when you speak!
Be silent and hear;
Inclining my cheek
And incredulous ear
To your voice, and command, and behest; hold your lightest wish
dear!

I am woman! But still
Am alive, and can feel
Every intimate thrill
That is woe or is weal:
I, aloof, and divided, apart, standing far, can I kneel?

Oh, if kneeling were right,
I should kneel nor be sad!
And abase in your sight
All the pride that I had!
I should come to you, hold to you, cling to you, call to you, glad!

If not, I shall know,
I shall surely find out!
And your world will throw
In disaster and rout!
I am woman, and glory, and beauty; I, mystery, terror and doubt!

I am separate still!
I am I and not you!
And my mind and my will,
As in secret they grew,
Still are secret; unreached, and untouched, and not subject to you.

A WOMAN IS A BRANCHY TREE

A woman is a branchy tree
And man a singing wind;
And from her branches carelessly
He takes what he can find:

Then wind and man go far away,
While winter comes with loneliness;
With cold, and rain, and slow decay,
On woman and on tree, till they

Droop to the earth again, and be
A withered woman, a withered tree;
While wind and man woo in the glade
Another tree, another maid.

NORA CRIONA

I have looked him round and looked him through,
Know everything that he will do

In such a case, and such a case;
And when a frown comes on his face

I dream of it, and when a smile
I trace its sources in a while.

He cannot do a thing but I
Peep to find the reason why;

For I love him, and I seek,
Every evening in the week,

To peep behind his frowning eye
With little query, little pry,

And make him, if a woman can,
Happier than any man.

—Yesterday he gripped her tight
And cut her throat. And serve her right!

SHAME

I was ashamed! I dared not lift my eyes!
I could not bear to look upon the skies!
What I had done! Sure, everybody knew!
From everywhere hands pointed where I stood,
And scornful eyes were piercing through and through
The moody armour of my hardihood!

I heard their voices too, each word an asp
That buzz'd and stung me sudden as a flame!
And all the world was jolting on my name!
And now and then there came a wicked rasp
Of laughter, jarring me to deeper shame!

And then I looked, and there was no one nigh!
No eyes that stabbed like swords or glinted sly!
No laughter creaking on the silent air!
—And then I saw that I was all alone
Facing my soul! And next I was aware
That this mad mockery was all my own!

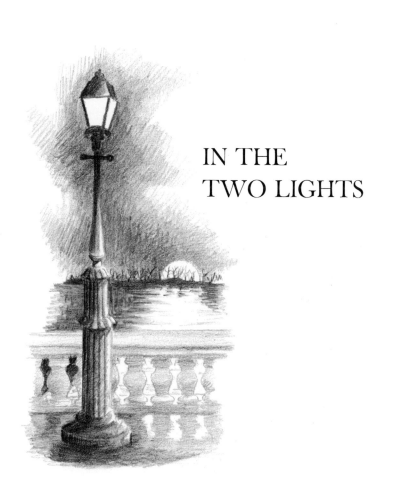

IN THE
TWO LIGHTS

HESPERUS

I

Upon the sky
Thy sober robes are spread;

They drape the twilight,
Veil on quiet veil;

Until the lingering daylight all has fled
Before thee, modest goddess, shadow-pale!

The hushed and reverent sky
Her diadem of stars has lighted high!

II

The lamb, the bleating kid, the tender fawn;
All that the sunburnt day has scattered wide,

Thou dost regather; holding, till the dawn,
Each flower and tree and beast unto thy side:

The sheep come to the pen;
And dreams come to the men;

And, to the mother's breast,
The tired children come, and take their rest.

III

Evening gathers everything
Scattered by the morning!

Fold for sheep, and nest for wing;
Evening gathers everything!

Child to mother, queen to king,
Running at thy warning!

Evening gathers everything
Scattered by the morning!

BLUE STARS AND GOLD

While walking through the trams and cars
I chanced to look up at the sky,
And saw that it was full of stars!

So starry-sown! A man could not
With any care, have stuck a pin
Through any single vacant spot.

And some were shining furiously;
And some were big and some were small;
But all were beautiful to see.

Blue stars and gold! A sky of grey!
The air between a velvet pall!
I could not take my eyes away!

And there I sang this little psalm
Most awkwardly! Because I was
Standing between a car and tram!

THE PAPS OF DANA

The mountains stand, and stare around,
They are far too proud to speak!

Altho' they are rooted in the ground,
Up they go—peak after peak,

Beyond the tallest house; and still
Climbing over tree and hill,

Until you'd think they'd never stop
Going up, top over top,

Into the clouds—Still I mark
That a linnet, or a lark,

Soaring just as high, can sing
As if he'd not done anything!

I think the mountains ought to be
Taught a little modesty!

THE WIND

The wind stood up, and gave a shout;
He whistled on his fingers, and

Kicked the withered leaves about,
And thumped the branches with his hand,

And said he'd kill, and kill, and kill;
And so he will! And so he will!

KATTY GOLLAGHER

[This is a small mountain outside Dublin]

The hill is bare! I only find
A stone, a sky, a twisted tree

Fighting on a bitter wind!
And that is all there is to see!

A tree, a hill, a wind, a sky,
Where nothing ever passes by!

WHITE FIELDS

I

In the winter time we go
Walking in the fields of snow;

Where there is no grass at all;
Where the top of every wall,

Every fence, and every tree,
Is as white as white can be.

II

Pointing out the way we came,
—Every one of them the same—

All across the fields there be
Prints in silver filigree;

And our mothers always know,
By the footprints in the snow,

Where it is the children go.

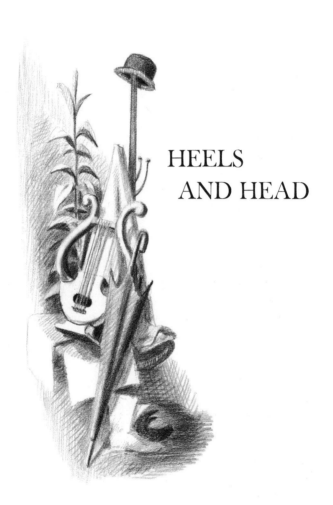

HEELS
AND HEAD

WHAT TOMAS SAID IN A PUB

I saw God! Do you doubt it?
Do you dare to doubt it?
I saw the Almighty Man! His hand
Was resting on a mountain! And
He looked upon the World, and all about it:
I saw Him plainer than you see me now
—You mustn't doubt it!

He was not satisfied!
His look was all dissatisfied!
His beard swung on a wind, far out of sight
Behind the world's curve! And there was light
Most fearful from His forehead! And He sighed—
—That star went always wrong, and from the start
I was dissatisfied!—

He lifted up His hand!
I say He heaved a dreadful hand
Over the spinning earth! Then I said,—Stay,
You must not strike it, God! I'm in the way!
And I will never move from where I stand!—
He said,—Dear child, I feared that you were dead,—
. . . And stayed His hand!

THE MARKET

A man said to me at the fair
—If you've got a poet's tongue
Tumble up and chant the air
That the Stars of Morning sung:

—I'll pay you, if you sing it nice,
A penny-piece.—I answered flat,
—Sixpence is the proper price
For a ballad such as that.—

But he stared and wagged his head,
Growling as he passed along
—Sixpence! Why, I'd see you dead
Before I pay that for a song.—

I saw him buy three pints of stout
With the sixpence—dirty lout!

BESSIE BOBTAIL

As down the road she wambled slow,
She had not got a place to go:
She had not got a place to fall
And rest herself—no place at all:
She stumped along, and wagged her pate;
And said a thing was desperate.

Her face was screwed and wrinkled tight
Just like a nut—and, left and right,
On either side, she wagged her head
And said a thing; and what she said
Was desperate as any word
That ever yet a person heard.

I walked behind her for a while,
And watched the people nudge and smile:
But ever, as she went, she said,
As left and right she swung her head,
—*Oh, God He knows! And, God He knows!*
And, surely God Almighty knows!

INDEPENDENCE

I grew single and sure,
And I will not endure
That my mind should be seen
By the sage or the boor.

I shall keep, if I can,
From each brotherly man:
The help of their hands
Is no part of my plan.

I will rise, I will go
To the land of my foe;
For his scowl is the sun
That shall cause me to grow.

WASHED IN SILVER

Gleaming in silver are the hills!
Blazing in silver is the sea!

And a silvery radiance spills
Where the moon drives royally!

Clad in silver tissue, I
March magnificently by!

THE FUR COAT

I walked out in my Coat of Pride;
I looked about on every side;

And said the mountains should not be
Just where they were, and that the sea

Was out of place, and that the beech
Should be an oak! And then, from each,

I turned in dignity, as if
They were not there! I sniffed a sniff;

And climbed upon my sunny shelf;
And sneezed a while; and scratched myself.

THE MERRY POLICEMAN

I was appointed guardian by
The Power that frowns along the sky,
To watch the Tree, and see that none
Plucked of the fruit that grew thereon.

There was a robber in the Tree,
Who climbed as high as ever he
Was able! At the top he knew
The Apple of all Apples grew.

The night was dark! The branch was thin!
In every wind he heard the din
Of angels calling—Guardian, see
That no man climbs upon the Tree—

But when he saw me standing there
He shook with terror and despair,
Then I said to him—Be at rest,
The best to him who wants the best—

So I was sacked! But I have got
A job in hell to keep me hot!

CROOKED-HEART

I loosed an arrow from my bow
Down into the world below;
Thinking— This will surely dart,
Guided by my guiding fate,
Into the malignant heart
Of the person whom I hate!

So, by hatred feathered well,
Swift the flashing arrow fell!
And I watched it from above
Disappear;
Cleaving sheer
Through the only heart I love!

Such the guard my angels keep!
But my foe is guarded well!
I have slain my love, and weep
Tears of blood! While he, asleep,
Does not know an arrow fell!

THE SECRET

I was frightened, for a wind
Crept along the grass, to say
Something that was in my mind
Yesterday—

Something that I did not know
Could be found out by the wind;
I had buried it so low
In my mind!

THE TWINS

Good and bad are in my heart,
But I cannot tell to you
—For they never are apart—
Which is better of the two.

I am this! I am the other!
And the devil is my brother;
But my father He is God!
And my mother is the Sod!
Therefore I am safe, you see,
Owing to my pedigree.

So I shelter love and hate
Like twin brothers in a nest;
Lest I find, when it's too late,
That the other was the best.

THE ANCIENT ELF

I am the maker,
The builder, the breaker,
The eagle-winged helper,
The speedy forsaker!

The lance and the lyre,
The water, the fire,
The tooth of oppression,
The lip of desire!

The snare and the wing,
The honey, the sting!
When you seek for me—look
For a different thing.

I, careless and gay,
Never mean what I say,
For my thoughts and my eyes
Look the opposite way!

EVERYTHING THAT I CAN SPY

Everything that I can spy
Through the circle of my eye;

Everything that I can see
Has been woven out of me!

I have sown the stars, and threw
Clouds of morn, and noon and eve

In the deeps and steeps of blue!
And all else that I perceive,

Sun and sea and mountain high,
Are made, are moulded by my eye!

Closing it, I do but find
Darkness, and a little wind.

IN THE POPPY FIELD

Mad Patsy said, he said to me,
That every morning he could see
An angel walking on the sky;
Across the sunny skies of morn
He threw great handfuls far and nigh
Of poppy seed among the corn;
—And then, he said, the angels run
To see the poppies in the sun—

—A poppy is a devil weed,—
I said to him—he disagreed:
He said the devil had no hand
In spreading flowers tall and fair
By corn and rye and meadow land,
And gurth and barrow everywhere:
The devil has not any flower,
But only money in his power.

And then he stretched out in the sun,
And rolled upon his back for fun!
He kicked his legs and roared for joy
Because the sun was shining down!
He said he was a little boy
And wouldn't work for any clown!
He ran and laughed behind a bee;
And danced for very ecstasy!

DANNY MURPHY

He was as old as old could be,
His little eye could hardly see,
His mouth was sunken in between
His nose and chin, and he was lean
And twisted up and withered quite,
So that he couldn't walk aright.

His pipe was always going out,
And then he'd have to search about
In all his pockets, and he'd mow
—O, deary me! and, musha now!—
And then he'd light his pipe, and then
He'd let it go clean out again.

He couldn't dance or jump or run,
Or ever have a bit of fun
Like me and Susan, when we shout
And jump and throw ourselves about:
—But when he laughed, then you could see
He was as young as young could be!

I WISH

I wish I had not come to man's estate,
I wish I was a silly urchin still,
With bounding pulses, and a heart elate
To meet whatever came of good or ill.

Of good or ill! Not knowing what was good,
But groping to a better than I knew;
And guessing deeper than I understood;
And hoping truths that seemed to be untrue.

Of good or ill! When so it often seems,
There is no good at all but only ill.
Alas, the sunny summer-time of dreams!
The dragons I had nerved my hand to kill!

The maid I could have rescued, and the queen
Whose champion long ago I might have been!

CHECK

The Night was creeping on the ground!
She crept, and did not make a sound

Until she reached the tree: And then
She covered it, and stole again

Along the grass beside the wall!
—I heard the rustling of her shawl

As she threw blackness everywhere
Along the sky, the ground, the air,

And in the room where I was hid!
But, no matter what she did

To everything that was without,
She could not put my candle out!

So I stared at the Night! And she
Stared back solemnly at me!

THE WHITE WINDOW

The Moon comes every night to peep
Through the window where I lie:
But I pretend to be asleep;
And watch the Moon go slowly by,
—And she never makes a sound!

She stands and stares! And then she goes
To the house that's next to me,
Stealing by on tippy-toes;
To peep at folk asleep maybe
—And she never makes a sound!

LESS THAN
DAINTILY

A GLASS OF BEER

The lanky hank of a she in the inn over there
Nearly killed me for asking the loan of a glass of beer;
May the devil grip the whey-faced slut by the hair,
And beat bad manners out of her skin for a year.

That parboiled ape, with the toughest jaw you will see
On virtue's path, and a voice that would rasp the dead,
Came roaring and raging the minute she looked at me,
And threw me out of the house on the back of my head!

If I asked her master he'd give me a cask a day;
But she, with the beer at hand, not a gill would arrange!
May she marry a ghost and bear him a kitten, and may
The High King of Glory permit her to get the mange.

THE GERALDINE'S CLOAK

I will not heed the message that you bring!
That loveliest lady gave her cloak to me;
And who'd believe she'd give away a thing
And ask it back again!—'Tis lunacy!

She knew that leaving her must make me grieve;
And for my going she had tender eyes!
. . . If some sweet angel sang it me, believe
I'd not believe that angel knew the skies!

The lovely Geraldine knows that the sting
Of want and woe is thrust deep into me:
I don't believe she'd do this kind of thing;
Nor treat a poet less than daintily!

IN THE IMPERATIVE MOOD

Let the man who has and doesn't give
Break his neck, and cease to live!

Let him who gives without a care
Gather rubies from the air!

WHEN YOU WALK

When you walk in a field,
Look down
Lest you trample
A daisy's crown!

But in a city
Look always high,
And watch
The beautiful clouds go by!

TO THE FOUR COURTS, PLEASE

The driver rubbed at his nettly chin
With a huge loose forefinger, crooked and black;
And his wobbly violet lips sucked in,
And puffed out again and hung down slack:
A black fang shone through his lop-sided smile,
In his little pouched eye flickered years of guile.

And the horse, poor beast! It was ribbed and forked;
And its ears hung down, and its eyes were old;
And its knees were knuckly; and, as we talked,
It swung the stiff neck that could scarcely hold
Its big skinny head up—then I stepped in,
And the driver climbed to his seat with a grin.

God help the horse, and the driver too!
And the people and beasts who have never a friend!
For the driver easily might have been you,
And the horse be me by a different end!
And nobody knows how their days will cease!
And the poor, when they're old, have little of peace!

WHAT THE TRAMP SAID

Why should we live when living is a pain?
I have not seen a flower had any scent,
Nor heard a bird sing once! The very rain
Seems dirty! And the clouds, all soiled and rent,
Toil sulkily across the black old sky;
And all the weary stars go moping by;
They care not whither—sea, or mount, or plain,
All's one—and what one gets is never gain!

The sun scowled yesterday a weary while,
That used to beam. The moon last night was grim
With cynic gaze, and frosty sullen smile:
And once I loved to gaze, while, from the rim
Of some great mountain, she would look, and gild
The rustling cornfield. Now she is filled
With bitterness and rancour sour as bile,
And blasts the world's surface every mile.

There is no more sunlight! All the weary world
Is steeped in shadow! And for evermore
The clouds will swarm and press, till I am hurled
Back to the heart of things! Oh, it is sore
And sad and sorry to be living! Let me die
And rest—while all eternity lolls by—
Where the fierce winds of God are closely furled
Ten million miles away from this damned world!

FROM HAWK AND KITE

Poor fluttered, frightened, silent one!
If we had seen your nest of clay,
We should have passed it, would have gone,
Nor frightened you away.

Are others too must guard a nest
From hawk, and kite, and secret foe,
And that despair is in their breast
Which you this moment know.

Shield the nests where'er they be!
In the house, or in the tree!
Guard the poor from treachery!

THE
GOLDEN BIRD

BESIDES THAT

If I could get to heaven
By eating all I could,
I'd become a pig,
And I'd gobble up my food!

Or, if I could get to heaven
By climbing up a tree,
I'd become a monkey,
And I'd climb up rapidly!

Or, if I could get to heaven
By any other way
Than the way that's told of,
I'd 'a been there yesterday!

But the way that we are told of
Bars the monkey and the pig!
And is very, very, difficult,
Besides that!

IRONY

Thus spake a man in days of old:
I will believe that God can be
The kind, the just, that we are told,
If He will throw down here to me
A bag of gold—

But when his wife rose from her bed
To see what kept her man away,
She found him, with a broken head:
And on the ground beside him lay
. . . A bag of lead!

THE BREATH OF LIFE

And while they talked and talked, and while they sat
Changing their base minds into baser coin;
And telling—they! how truth and beauty join,
And how a certain this was good, but that
Was baser than the viper or the toad,
Or the blind beggar glaring down the road;

I turned from them in fury, and I ran
To where the moon shone out upon the height,
Down the long reaches of a summer night
Stretching slim fingers, and the starry clan
Grew thicker than the flowers that we see
Clustered in quiet fields of greenery.

The quietudes that sunder star from star;
The hazy distances of loneliness,
Where never eagle's wing, or timid press
Of lark or wren could venture; and the far
Profundities untroubled and unstirred
By any act of man or thought or word;

These held me with amazement and delight!
I yearned up through the spaces of the sky,
Beyond the rolling clouds, beyond the high

And delicate white moon, and up the height,
And past the rocking stars, and out to where
The aether failed in spaces sharp and bare.

The Breath that is the very Breath of Life
Throbbed close to me! I heard the pulses beat,
That lift the universes into heat!
The slow withdrawal, and the deeper strife
Of His wide respiration—like a sea
It ebbed and flooded through immensity.

The Breath of Life, in wave on mighty wave!
O moon and stars, swell to a raptured song!
Ye mountains, toss the harmony along!
O little men, with little souls to save,
Swing up glad chauntings! Ring the skies above
With boundless gratitude for boundless love!

Probing the ocean to its steepest drop!
Rejoicing in the viper and the toad;
And the blind beggar glaring down the road;
And they, who talk and talk and never stop,
Equally quickening! With a care to bend
The gnat's slant wing into a swifter end.

       .   .   .

The silence clung about me like a gift!
The tender night-time folded me around
Protectingly! And, in a peace profound,
The clouds drooped slowly backward, drift on drift
Into the darkness; and the moon was gone;
And soon the stars had vanished, every one.

But on the sky, a hand's-breadth in the west,
A faint cold radiance crept, and soared, and spread;

Until the rustling heavens overhead,
And the grey trees, and grass, were manifest:
Then, through the chill, a golden spear was hurled,
And the great sun tossed laughter on the world!

THE VOICE OF GOD

I bent again unto the ground
And I heard the quiet sound
Which the grasses make when they
Come up laughing from the clay.

—We are the voice of God!—they said:
Thereupon I bent my head
Down again that I might see
If they truly spoke to me.

But, around me, everywhere,
Grass and tree and mountain were
Thundering in mighty glee,
—We are the voice of deity!—

And I leapt from where I lay:
I danced upon the laughing clay:
And, to the rock that sang beside,
—We are the voice of God!—I cried.

ON A REED

1

I have a reed of oaten straw,
I play upon it when I may;
And the music that I draw
Is as happy as the day.

It has seven holes, and I
Play it high, and play it low;
I can make it laugh, or cry,
Can make or banish joy or woe.

Any song that you can name
I will play it on the word;
Old or new is all the same,
I'm as ready as a bird.

2

But there is a tune, and though
I try to play it, day and night,
Blowing high, and blowing low,
I can never play it right!

I know it well, without a flaw,
The tune that yet I cannot play
On my reed of oaten straw,
Though I practise night and day!

Penny pipe, be good to me!
And play the tune I want to play,
Or I will smash you on a tree,
And throw your wicked halves away!

IF I HAD WINGS
JUST LIKE A BIRD

If I had wings just like a bird
I would not say a single word;
I'd spread my wings, and fly away
Beyond the reach of yesterday!

If I could swim just like a fish
I'd give my little tail a swish;
I'd swim ten days and nights, and then
I never would be found again!

Or, if I were a comet bright,
I'd drop in secret every night
Ten million miles! And no one would
Know where I kept my solitude!

But I am not a bird, or fish,
Or comet; so I need not wish:
And need not try to get away
Beyond the reach of yesterday.

Damn yesterday! And this and that,
And these and those! And all the flat,
Dull catalogue of weighty things
That somehow fasten to my wings!

Over the pine trees, and the mountain top!
Never to stop lifting wide wings!
To fly, and fly, and fly
Into the sky!

HATE

My enemy came nigh;
And I
Stared fiercely in his face:
My lips went writhing back in a grimace,
And stern I watched him from a narrowed eye:

Then, as I turned away,
My enemy,
That bitter-heart, and savage, said to me:

—Some day, when this is past;
When all the arrows that we have are cast;
We may ask one another why we hate,
And fail to find a story to relate:
It may seem to us, then, a mystery
That we could hate each other—
Thus said he; and did not turn away;
Waiting to hear what I might have to say!

But I fled quickly: fearing, if I stayed,
I might have kissed him, as I would a maid.

SOFT WINGS

I saw a beggar woman bare
Her bosom to the winter air,
And into the tender nest
Of her famished mother-breast
She laid her child;
And him beguiled,
With crooning song, into his rest.

With crooning song, and tender word,
About a little singing bird,
That spread soft wings about her brood!
And tore her bosom for their food!
And sang the while,
Them to beguile,
All in the forest's solitude!

And, hearing this, I could not see
That she was clad in misery!
For in her heart there was a glow
Warmed her bare feet in the snow!
In her heart was hid a sun
Would warm a world for every one!

IN WASTE PLACES

As a naked man I go
Through the desert, sore afraid;
Holding high my head, although
I'm as frightened as a maid.

The lion crouches there! I saw
In barren rocks his amber eye!
He parts the cactus with his paw!
He stares at me, as I go by!

He would pad upon my trace
If he thought I was afraid!
If he knew my hardy face
Veils the terrors of a maid.

He rises in the night-time, and
He stretches forth! He snuffs the air!
He roars! He leaps along the sand!
He creeps! He watches everywhere!

His burning eyes, his eyes of bale
Through the darkness I can see!
He lashes fiercely with his tail!
He makes again to spring at me!

I am the lion, and his lair!
I am the fear that frightens me!
I am the desert of despair!
And the night of agony!

Night or day, whate'er befall,
I must walk that desert land,
Until I dare my fear, and call
The lion out to lick my hand!

THE GOLDEN BIRD

If Joy, the Golden Bird, would fly,
Do not close an hand upon her!
She belongeth to the sky,
With all the winds of heaven on her:
Only when her wings are free
Bird of Lovely Life is she.

He who Joy of Life would store,
Heart of his be widely open;
Throw the key out with the door,
Throw the hope out with the hopen:
Give her—as she finds in sky—
Place to dip, and soar, and fly.

She will come again, I wist!
She of thee shall not be frighted!
She shall sing upon thy fist!
By her shall thy dark be lighted!
By her freedom thou art given
Right and room in joyous heaven!

THE ROSE ON THE WIND

Dip and swing!
Lift and sway!
Dream a life
In a dream, away!

Like a dream
In a sleep
Is the rose
On the wind!

And a fish
In the deep;
And a man
In the mind!

Dreaming to lack
All that is his!
Dreaming to gain
All that he is!

Dreaming a life,
In a dream, away!
Dip and swing!
Lift and sway!

ON A LONELY SPRAY

Under a lonely sky, a lonely tree
Is beautiful! All that is loneliness
Is beautiful! A feather, lost at sea;
A staring owl; a moth; a yellow tress
Of seaweed on a rock, is beautiful!

The night-lit moon, wide-wandering in sky!
A blue-bright spark, where ne'er a cloud is up!
A wing, where no wing is, it is so high!
A bee in winter! And a buttercup,
Late blown! are lonely, and are beautiful!

She whom you saw but once, and saw no more!
That he who startled you, and went away!
The eye that watched you from a cottage door!
The first leaf, and the last! The break of day!
The mouse, the cuckoo, and the cloud, are beautiful!

For all that is, is lonely! All that may
Will be as lonely as is that you see!
The lonely heart sings on a lonely spray!
The lonely soul swings lonely in the sea!
And all that loneliness is beautiful!

All: all alone: and all without a part
Is beautiful! For beauty is all-where!
Where is an eye, is beauty! Where an heart,
Is beauty, breathing out on empty air,
All that is lonely, and is beautiful!

THE PETAL OF A ROSE

Let us be quiet for a while,
The morrow comes! Let us be still!
Let us close our eyes and smile,
Knowing that the morrow will

Come as certain as the sun
Or a sorrow! Let us be
Peaceful till this night be done!
And we rise again to see

That the thing is not in view!
That the memory is gone!
That the world is made anew
Different for every one!

Different! The morrow glows
Where the black wings spread and brood,
Where the petal of a rose
Blushes in the solitude!

DEATH

Slow creatures, slow,
Nuzzle and press,
And take their food
In the darkness!

No stir is now
In all that once was all!
No dream; no sound;
No sight; no sense is there!

Unseen, the beam of the sun!
Unknown, the ring of the light!
Unknown, in the cave!
Unseen, by the slow, slow, hungers!

Naught's left
—But food!
All else, that was,
Is away!

—Far away
In the Gleam!
In the Ring!
In the Beam!
In the Sun!

THE PIT OF BLISS

When I was young
I dared to sing
Of everything,
And anything!
Of Joy, and woe, and fate, and God!
Of dreaming cloud, and teeming sod!
Of hill that thrust an amber spear
In the sunset! And the sheer
Precipice that shakes the soul
To its black gape—I sang the whole
Of God and Man, nor sought to know
Man or God, or Joy, or Woe!
And, though an older wight I be,
My soul hath still such Ecstasy
That, on a pulse, I sing and sing
Of Everything, and Anything!

2

There is a Light
Shines in the head:
It is not gold,
It is not red,

But, as the lightning's blinding light,
It is a stare of silver white
That one surmise might fancy blue!
On that, mind-blinding, hue I gaze
An instant, and am in a maze
Of thinking—could one call it so?
It is no thinking that I know!
—An hurricane of Knowing, that
Could whelm the soul that was not pat
To flinch, and lose the deadly thing;
—And Sing, and Sing again, and Sing
Of Everything, and Anything!

3

An Eagle
Whirling up the sky;
Sunblind! Dizzy!
Urging high,
And higher beating yet a wing,
Until he can no longer cling,
Or hold; or do a thing, but fall,
And sink, and whirl, and scream, through all
His dizzy, heaven-hell of Pit,
In mile-a-minute flight from It
That he had dared! From height of height,
So the Poet takes his flight
And tumble in the Pit of Bliss!
And, in the roar of that Abyss,
And falling, he will Sing and Sing
Of Everything, and Anything!

4

What is Knowing?
'Tis to see!
What is Feeling?
'Tis to be!

What is Love? But, more and more,
To See and Be! To be a Pour
And Avalanche of Being, till
Being ceases, and is still
For very motion—What is Joy?
—Being, past all earthly cloy
And intermixture! Being spun
Of Itself is Being won!
That is Joy—And this is God,
To be That, in cloud and clod:
And, in cloud, and clod, to Sing
Of Everything, and Anything!

MISCELLANY

SARASVATI

As bird to nest, when, moodily,
The storm-cloud murmurs nigh the tree,
Thus let him flee,
Who can to sing,
Here hath he calm, and sheltering.

As bee to hive, when, with the sun,
Long honey-gathering is done,
Who can to sing,
There let him flee,
This is his cell, his companie.

As child to mother running, where
The thunder shudders through the air,
Thus let him flee,
Who can to sing,
Here hath he ward, and cherishing.

Fly to thy talent? To thy charm!
Thy nest, thine hive, thy sheltering arm!
Who can to sing,
There let him flee,
This is, naught else is, certainty.

From THEME AND VARIATIONS

THEME

The golden eve is all astir,
And tides of sunset flood on us
—Incredible, miraculous—
We look with adoration on
Beauty coming, beauty gone,
That waits not any looking on.

Thoughts will bubble up, and break,
Spilling a sea, a limpid lake,
Into the soul; and, as they go
—Lightning visitors! we know
A lattice opened, and the mind
Poised for all that is behind
The lattice, and the poising mind.

Could the memory but hold!
—All the sunsets, flushed with gold,
Are streaming in it!

All the store
Of all that ever was before
Is teeming in it!

All the wit
Of holy living, holy writ,

Waiting till we remember it,
Is dreaming in it!

VARIATIONS

8

The small, green leaf
Fell down from the tree:

And the great oak tree
Fell down from the cliff:

And the huge, hard cliff
Slipped down to the sea:

And the sea was sucked
To the sun in a whiff:

Then . . . blink!
And a shout!

And the sun
Blew out . . .

9

No bees, no leaves:
No carollings sung:
No linnets in the eaves,
No young!

Ice, deep in the dale:
Ice, thick in the wold:
Ice, white in the vale:
Ice-cold!

Ice, trapped in ice!
—Oh foolish fear!
For the south blows spice,
And the rose is seen,

And the lark
Is here,
And the woods
Are green!

13

Fear is, where is no cause!
To this, all-dark,
The small child comes
A-wearying of the day:
And the bird
—Sight-tired, light-weary, sun-sick—
Seeks here his sleep at dark'ning evenfall:
Glad to relinquish space and aery-light:
Glad to forget—and to forget he can!
The too-seen, and the too-known,
In the better-known,
In the first-known,
In the deep-dark!

I AM WRITER

I am writer,
And do know
Nothing that is false,
Or true:

Have only care
To take it so,
And make it sing,
And make it new:

And make it new,
And make it sing,
When, if it's pleasing
Unto you,

Say, I've done
A useful thing
—As your servant
Ought to do.

IN THE RED

When I was young
I had no sense
—Now I'm older
None have I:

I had no fiddle,
Had no pence
—Now I'm older
None have I:

There was no tune
That I could play
—Now I'm older
None play I:

But, over the hills,
And far away!
—Now I'm older
There am I.

FROM *THEME WITH VARIATIONS*

No pride hath he who sings of escape from love:
All songs of escape from love are songs of despair:
Who so hath gat him away hath got nowhere.

He sings below all that he knows as above:
He hath no mind for the gentle, heart for the fair:
No pride hath he who sings of escape from love:
All songs of escape from love are songs of despair.

Who doth not sing as the wild-dove sings to the dove,
The night-wild sprite to the moon, of love is bare:
He knows not pity, passion, praise, nor prayer:

No pride hath he who sings of escape from love:
All songs of escape from love are songs of despair:
Who so hath gat him away hath got nowhere.

MIDNIGHT

AFTER SAPPHO

Fainter and thin,
The lapsing moon has paled
From the rough sky:
The Pleiades have sailed,
Star after star,
Bending a silver mast
Into the darkness:
And the hollow vast
Of heaven clangs
Where a trumpet-wind is blown!
The hour goes, and is gone,
—I sleep alone.

DOFFING THE BONNET

Informed, precise, empowered, the seed
Knows present work, and future need:
Knows airlessness . . . and dreams of air!
Knows from the Dense and Dark to where
The Sun doth conjure all, and bless
Knowledge and Will with fruitfulness.

Ere she will let them from the dark,
All motherly, with shields of bark
She wraps each tendril in a skein
From the cold wind, and the cold rain,
From deadening doubt and dead delay,
From the hard stone and the harsh clay.

Deep in the dark, with rooty tongue,
She, knowing, seeks all things among;
With knowledge science never had
She knows the good, she knows the bad:
Chemist and Sage and Prophet, she,
The Finite, plans Infinity.

She springs the branch, she weights the bough,
She shapes the leaf—and she knows how
T'infuse a delicate, a sweet

—Distillation complex, neat—
That the quick bee, Love's Messenger,
May carry Life that's Soul of her.

.   .   .

Bow a little to the seed
That knows so much, and hath no need
But soil and dew and a warm ray
From the bright smile that wakes the day
—Alone! Not lonely! Not afraid!
Bow to the Seed that the Seed made.

INDEX TO FIRST LINES